RAGGED DISCLOSURES

RAGGED DISCLOSURES

PAUL HETHERINGTON

RECENT
WORK
PRESS

Ragged Disclosures
Recent Work Press
Canberra, Australia

Copyright © Paul Hetherington, 2022

ISBN: 9780645356328 (paperback)

A catalogue record for this
book is available from the
National Library of Australia

Cover image: Dan Cristian Padure via unplash
Cover design: Recent Work Press
Set by Recent Work Press

recentworkpress.com

ss

For Michelle

Contents

Trove

Isolations

Manoeuvres

Sand

The Arms Remember

Ragged Disclosures 1

At a Roman bar they sit close, as words tug like magnets. She unfolds a story about an Australian farm and 'childhood happiness'. At three a.m. he wakes and sends a text—after an insomniac bulkiness dredges his life and grey sands rise. In the morning her reply pings softly—they'll meet for breakfast and visit the cinema. Movies he's seen run through thought as consciousness stumbles—as if down a hillside slippery with pebbles.

She decides to move in and he concurs—'for four months only'— though both agree they're badly suited. They say they'll travel, enjoy conversation, write and make love, but they're wrapped in truncation—every plan resists a future. Occasionally she asks, 'What are we doing?' But she enjoys the lack of commitment and 'our dedication to the body'. She scoffs when he says, 'perhaps we should marry'. He nods when she says, 'careful—I might agree.'

It's as if they speak contrasting languages despite their shared Australian vernacular. She enjoys new films and the internet; he returns to books and classical music. She listens to Handel with a curling lip, but eventually agrees it's comforting— 'that sweetness of sound'. She proffers details about her past life, but much is unclear. He decides not to press her as she resists disclosure. Their ragged intersections make an unjoined, searching rapport.

HOME, AWAY

Home: Beginning

The journey's beginning was not the road from the city, where a man dressed as a woman offered orange cordial. It was not the road where a couple with a child slowed their station wagon. It was much later, on the side of a Victorian cliff, standing in front of a ruined museum—when you saw the ghosts. They spoke to each other in the breeze's murmur—of cities where murder was committed; of vast markets where dangles of jewellery made a tinkering music; of houses sculpted from mountains' faces. Their windows stared over a long drop into a red valley. They were telling you about yourself. You felt fingers locking with your own; arms shepherding you away. You stood apart, seeing a wombat digging nearby, and a farmer spraying yellow poison in a field. The ghosts murmured until you had made ten kilometres.

Away: Bodies

We are solitary bodies on either side of the small world. We jealously hold our self-possession, like children grasping their blankets at a school camp. Years have carried us through *mise en scènes* we barely recollect—we occupy their aftermath. Such fragments we collect, on a white blanket of shoreline; and views of sculpture, that step toward us in ancient galleries; and rancorous gatherings of car fumes and columns. Here, as we taste black espresso like water from the underworld, a motor ratchets and coughs. Our destination is a word turned in the mouth. The map between us shows a coastline's ragged hand.

Home: The Word on Our Lips

The word on our lips is 'fire', pushing smoke through the hills, sullying our conception of place. As winds increase, we fear an inferno; as we struggle through conversation we keep returning to the wind. Animals congregate at the dam; lightning drily hammers the valley. We demand rain from the mountain and when it comes it's a muffled incantation, then a flurry of animals. We see smoke scrubbed from the sky and remember a woman we loved saying incomprehensible things about weather. That was another season, when summer closed our eyes; when old gods cavorted in our language. We were young and naked under a sun shower's playful fingers.

Away: Basket

We might be slow light that sinuously climbs the columns; we hear gulls calling and the insouciance of wind. Overlooking a vast topography of hills, green touches thought. We imagine the landscape to be something written—long ago; a lost mythology. We, too, become more like words; an entwining of grammar, as you ask me to speak for you. Yet, when you do, the sentence drifts, carrying me toward isolation. There's an ancient statue dug from a wide field. Clods decorate the bronze, which examines modernity with an obsidian gaze. Women nurse vegetables in gathers of long skirts, their words incisive as cut stone. As you lift a basket of broccoli your arms lengthen like sunshine.

Home: Trumpeter

The trumpeter shouts a hole into the world. Long notes, a window looking out to a man hugging himself at the edge of a bay; a turbulence like hands wringing saturated air. The past recurs, in the form of a gangly child. He has examined the sky time and again, as a kicked football dives toward his grasp. To hold, as if motion itself may be stilled. To keep an idea aloft, no matter how often it empties from clouds. And here's a long note, like a dirge. Dark music gathers and runs like the river Lethe.

Away: Geometries

At dawn, I find again the rectangles and triangles that had haunted me—a view of a medieval town in England after climbing three hundred steps. You accompany me, and behind us a ruined cathedral splits into perpendiculars and fractals; gravestones scratch the air. The tower might once have trapped Rapunzel; I see a woman dragging her sheet and long hair across an expansive tangle of a bed, her body turning like a dancer. She offers a chilly glass and light runs like liquid down the stem. Marriage as twelve years or eight wanton centuries. A tower fixing light's geometries.

Home: Tablets

Absence triangulates longing and we know ourselves through repeated words—incised in space as if on Akkadian tablets. We imagine ourselves dressed in the habits of that empire, and it feels strangely close—as if longings might transgress centuries; as if feelings channel us toward alien cultures. The gap stretches into unimagined shapes; our beliefs adopt sketches of new emotion. We become formal and estranged, like figures on stone. Our present is skinned. The far edge of absence washes with millennia of sand.

Away: Estuary

My heart tin-taps its way across a yellow estuary.
Waterbirds scream and launch through spillages;
shatterings of thought fall like fists of rain. Width,
light and abstractions weigh with the import of a
longer journey—when we were in Rome, traipsing
the cobbles. Your voice shines suddenly, like a
cathedral slant, and I see a stream encircling St.
Peter's. The pope is speaking to a massed crowd and
gargoyles utter their prayers in rivulets. The estuary's
birds are crying, 'Out of reach'.

Home: Next Door

We climb through a sash window, shoes clattering onto wooden boards. Our neighbour has gone but the house still holds her impeccably tucked bed and decades of rigid photographs. Last week she greeted us with a handshake. Dust blues the air. There's a sense of the recently living stooping under the tide of being; obscurity lifting like smoke. We tug at ribbon-wrapped letters, a note about 'remembering the recorder'. How do we say that we might have loved her as we trespass on unsanctioned feeling?

Away: Unripe

You speak of the last king of Cumbria, and at
Dunmail Raise the roadway skirts a pile of stones.
Legend insists he'll return, but time is always unripe,
history's longer view obscured among billboards
and headlines. We walk where literature was made,
hearing the bleating of sheep and the rotor of a
helicopter. We hearken to the nineteenth century—
but on the ferry and next to the freeway, no birds
sing.

Ragged Disclosures 2

*His complex grammar makes little
impression on her—stubborn action's
already spoken and subsequent
sentences merely say what's occurred.
Pressing him, she insists on the unlikely
and oblique, where words won't always
follow; where language has no
immediate scaffold. In darkness, hands
and eyes find shapes of waists and legs,
squeezing toward a surlier knowledge
than language recognises, carousing
with the wild other.*

*For those hours there's no way to name
desire—as if words already missed
their chance; as if what they do trumps
every noun and verb. Later, bathing
him in mellifluousness, she insists on
speaking's strange hypnosis, that
stymies action—where the intimacy of
bodies is a thousand times refracted.
Yet verbs and nouns, as if in water,
swim near shapes of waists, squeezing
and diving toward expressiveness.*

*'Yes,' she says, affirming a way
through doubt's negations—as if their
debate misses the point. Outlining
suggestions, her voice becomes a kind
of prayer, and he, her close disciple.
They find a language-lit entrancement,
where the power of words lies in saying
little. Sentences give way to reaching
arms. Touch is the untidy speech they
harness, yoked by legs and sucking kisses.
She tells him something that
might be her name, but he fails to
listen.*

SLIPPAGES

Screen

1.
Meetings, construals, broken words.　　　　One member says she'll be signing off soon; a painting wobbles, a　　　bike merges into a wall. Words climb to a near-falsetto. Outside,　　　　someone's radio says we're reaching the right level of flattening, as the number　　　of dead increases. I think of cremating my father; how he died too soon　　　to be one of these statistics, his body underneath my stalling gaze. Like children,　　　we do not know what we understand.

2.
You phone to say, 'Despite isolation,　　　I'm doing my best'. Soon I'm in a meeting that shatters into mask-like　　　faces. I've muted audio; a few voices compete for electronic　　　space,　　discussing　　　'what-we-all-can-certainly-achieve'. It's a way of　　　surviving when verities are worth little and the plagues are suddenly new.　　　Public figures offer consolation like secular forms of prayer. Yet our gods have　　　left, as rivers flood or vanish. You phone, asking loudly what you can possibly do.

3.
How do we disappear so quickly into　　　this weird notion of ourselves? The screen asks for a password. In another　　　age we might have entered a secret wardrobe or yard where innocence is　　　eventually found out. In a different year, we may have gathered ourselves into　　　a broad idea of travel. Today, we take our virtual presence across suburbs, to　　　share glimpses of ordinary rooms. No poems start; no *Dawn Treader* quivers.

4.
The flesh is　　　facsimile. We cannot read the age-old bodily signs that we evolved to understand.　　　Your embrace sits in imagination; we close down screens. Walls creak, and when　　your phone call comes from quarantine I think of eloquent hands. You talk of　　　'seven more impossible days' and I remember the Sagrada Família—walking under its unfinished roof.　　　Sky collapsed as spires stood apart.

Firebreak

We cross the fuming line where a creek edges
oaks. Heat bounces and slides, like a ghostly
skateboarder. You picture salving words
riding on a breeze—but what could they be?
We push past untidy oleanders.

Hills are broken beads flung at the distance,
lightning strikes bushland. Nearby, a
farmhouse crouches into threads of smoke;
burrows punctuate the ground. We walk the
boundary and you sob. Over following
weeks we broach the fenceline, replanting
native trees. Wallabies and parrots crowd;
yelps gather the yard.

Sometimes you stand in the shallow dam
pushing palms toward meagre rain, pressing
fingers into soil, shouting at tree and star. At
the boundary we know what's behind us, and
what we believed was ours. You point at a
wattle throwing flowers like confetti
smatterings.

Underneath the stretched clothesline a lizard
sips from a bowl as you talk of the medieval
mystery plays—'fables,' you say, 'when fear
was abroad.' We try the plays' language—
sentences that swirl with archaic sounds and
are stolen by the wind.

Ghost

1.

You fix the house. Six months with claw hammer, joists, plasterboard, corrugated iron. A month more with cornices, skirting boards, ceiling roses and grout—tidying up, making good. You place a mirror in the hallway, hang framed Hokusai prints in other rooms. At last, you lie down.

2.

A voice says 'father'. You see dry hills hanging in the mirror; a river purling with blood-red water. Trees scrabble at earth, like hands; a sky drops murk. The voice says 'go' as clearly as your clock ticks.

3.

Your father peers from the mirror even as you tuck your shirt and walk outside to release the hens. There's hesitancy in your language as you wonder what nouns and verbs might represent this life.

4.

You have few lucid memories but there are sensations as if the sky touches your skin and the river bruises your eyes, as if the corrugations in the nearby ridge have been gouged by sentences your father spoke—that the landscape refuses and wind disperses.

In These Closed Rooms

1.

Buildings congregate on flat land near the river. Only
months ago the place was empty: marshes where we
went barefoot as children in a green world—rough-
hewn days, like notched spears we tore from
branches, building fires, making incursions. We
tested our meagre strength against a rising miasma.
Now, these long encampments are cleaned, no matter
that they're new.

2.

Locked down, we think of boarding ships that gather
the Mediterranean. Old notions fish at us, pulling us
from sleep to cobbled alleys—a woman in the market
offering lemons; a man banging espressos on a
counter.

3.

The reruns begin to tire: so many detectives finding
out murderous truths as criminals confess—like
Raskolnikov, they're unable to bear the schismatic
weight of being. Reading aloud the Penguin *Horace*
is a way into urbanity, until we imagine gladiatorial
games where slaves replay the sack of Carthage. The
thought nestles like a contemporary rat: 'If you lift
your upturned palms to the sky.' No place escapes
tainted language.

Caravel

1.

Breakers dig at limestone cliffs, as if levering pearls.
'Turn the key twice,' you say as we cross the
headland. 'Ease it gently.' Shutters are clamped; a
creeper hangs berries, like decorations; tendrils
deform the window frame. Words return, that
floated and sang three summers ago: 'beachhead',
'seafowl', 'reef'. We talk of 'adventurers' who brought
mayhem, written as romantic tales.

2.

Waves stand as wind cuts their tops, stretching
syllables. We patch walls and roof, bring furniture,
stand in rooms as if to possess them. The cottage
belongs to an older time—its dry twistings remind
us.

3.

We find ourselves speaking in subdued voices,
imbibing meanings from middens, rockface and
paddock. You point to the fence line that falls
raggedly down a cliff-face, walking on the top,
imagining a caravel with guns, unfurling lateen
sails.

Dial

1. In the space between
    death and grief's final onset, memory's gears
fail—a second hand ratchets and won't shift.
Hesitations multiply; words stall under thought's
glare.

2. There's a cobbled square
        where we stood like penitents years ago,
facing obliquity that's now strained in thought—a
wedge of purposelessness.

3. Past tense and future tense
        are trapped in the twitch of a clock's hand.

4. Although we're dressed
        in time's sumptuousness, the niggling clock
begins to move with precise, pin-hands—once we
were transfixed as they pushed each of us through
childhood.

5. Grief folds and skids,
        like a black-and-white celluloid film spilling
on a floor. We fail to lift the cascading images.

Sand and Ash

1.

A woman who died eight years ago steps onto Viale Aurelio
Saffi in Rome. There are half-sunk cobbles where she leans
into sunshine, raising her hand. Time shoves the body,
streets dispossess ——

2.

Blown sand camouflages the dune's low scrub, scratching
eyes and enlarging a scarf. Where you've dug, it skates and
elevates, just as the tide extends a yawn of water; just as
your mother's voice flails like blown cotton. It bulges in this
stride of memory, flying toward the coastline as crabs seethe
——

3.

Within a train's tunnelling motion, spoons jiggle on teacups,
a dark voice yells, lamplight flattens furniture. Five men
are talking, slipping fingers through a tabletop's spilled beer
——

4.

All day you see apartments and houses rising, and roadways
jagging through 'reclaimed' wilderness, as insects
congregate. All night you're a fugitive in phantasmagoric
dark, living in marshlands west of the city, trapping birds,
fingering scant berries ——

5.

It's an unwieldy species of sadness that sees a baboon falling
into a clearing; a lake that siphons away in slaps and sprawls
of mud; a woman shouting about losing her father
——

6.

In the burning, the shed goes first and then the dog kennel.
A howl lathers fields. Imploding, the house becomes a wide
tent of embers. Three men lie on grass, another falls into a
stream like a fuming cinder. A belatedness of late rain on ash

Jetty and Eels

Stepping back, listening to the cuff of the river, and oars; hearing timbers jar and push; bailing water; interlocking fingers—an aubergine nail polish—and words spinning like a cataract of leaves. Her beauty crashes on your eyes, and awkwardness; she says the season is imperceptibly shifting. Her word, 'bereft'—//

stepping ashore, pulled toward one another, a lugging sensation, but the drag of words won't catch it as water quickens—a jetty, banging boards, a cry.

*

You hold a girl's hand in the bearded lady's tent, wondering at the bust her beard nearly touches and the girl's hooking fingers. She disentangles herself before the sideshow's open-mouthed clowns, and you might be one of them, gawking at the unreal//

this 'tour of ancient monuments'. There's a view of currents like dark eels; a dispute about the clash of armies; a lift and jolt, blue diesel fumes. You peer, laced froth disperses and the river quietens. An old fort rises: bricks, broken paths, a well—vestiges of empire. You imagine a girl in that faraway time, drawing water. It seems possible to place your hand on her shoulder. She passes a bucket—brimmingly, teeteringly full.

Francis Bacon Triptych

A sweep of pigments, standing near hospital grounds, finding in his body unwieldy gobs of surrealism. In this puzzle of light, buildings fall into recollections of other paintings. Has de Chirico walked here? Windows lean inwards

as an intractable cage of lines. Your father's words were slashes of red. Accompanying Nanny Lightfoot, being horsewhipped by the Captain's grooms, learning roulette, boyhood's stretched and sketchy feeling saw you pacing up and down, as in a gallery, watching your lacerations become more and more aesthetic

as in Poussin's *Massacre* or some scene of *Crucifixion*. Over time the wounds lost their rawness and you stepped back like a connoisseur, staring hard at the morning's mirror, not recognising your face's brushed, clean lines. You tipped water over the glass, disappearing in its blur and fall. *That's me*, you thought, somewhere fading into absence. Almost unrecognisably, your gaze returned.

Winged Catechisms

1.

You find yourself talking to the wind

as if it carries grave propositions. Thoughts attach to your body like wings—you feel a shudder and lift. Soon you're mouthing gnomic phrases—each one as evanescent as the trail of breath on glass—and, afterwards, you can't remember the words, as if persuasive images reduce to oily glints. A sense of the disconsolate ushers in the dead, reminding you they never finish talking. Words dissolve in air like fragments of catechism.

2.

A woman stands on another's shoulders,

as if supported by outspread wings; a man carries a wrapped baby and gathers coins in a cup. The city's cathedral breaks in multifaceted window light. Recollection shows a girl reading under a peppermint tree and a drama class's rowdiness in a weatherboard church; a man on a bicycle spilling small change from his pocket. As a girl reaches to gather the silver tricklings, a boy challenges her with scrabbling fingers. In a small room, disentanglings—a dropped blouse, an unshuttered window, the stretched sound of a bell encircling belief.

3.

The window looks onto an angel

standing in the square. Her skin is marble white; her gestures are flurries, like the wing beats of small birds. The sky's an overflow of starlight; words populate the apartment block like a swarm. A man reads to a woman from a blank book; they are veiled in each other's gaze. The angel's mouth babbles with human speech.

Ragged Disclosures 3

As if they'd passed each other in the street without recognition—both of them felt the mood fall like the bluest afternoon. But she lifted it by speaking, before throwing her head back and shaking her hair—'my volcanic feelings'—grabbing a towel and heading to the shower. Later that evening, they sat together in a state she called 'my second honeymoon'. A movie played, showing black-and-white characters in a complex mime.

There's no way to secure memory—as if the past's already vanishing into fiction. Yet he remembers the hallway where she pressed him between the wall's cool plaster and her skin. It was so hot outside, the air's glints beaded like a curtain as her body's flame tongued his flesh. Her whispered words were incendiary, as if minutes were the apex of being burningly alive—or so language tried to say, flammable in wonderment.

'No,' she said, refusing the suggestion of going out for coffee. They talked of literature and he recalled words from a favourite novel: 'We will hold ourselves to each other's avowals.' She nodded: 'We know the unruliness of language, and unhappiness, yet we persist.' 'Coffee?' he asked and, as he moved toward the door, she intercepted him.

THIS DELICIOUS FAILURE
OF COMMON NAMES

Summer

Time skirts a property's perimeters, where you consider years of herding and fencing. And a swing rocks over the creek as fractures of shade and sunlight churn underneath silky oaks; as a boy bends a sapling to the earth and tries to bury its end, piling rocks to secure it. He steps back and it shudders upright; you step forward into the space he's made, where light breaks through shattered foliage. He absconds, red-faced at your words; you move half into shade, possessing yourself against his intrusion. The thrill of light breaks over your arm. You see streaks of sweat, holding teetering summer in your palm.

Triangles

Triangles chime in the hands of boys and girls. Tall windows scatter dusty light. At lunchtime the headmaster is beaten at table tennis by one of the boys. A line of sentences is chalked on the board; a lesson on verbs and adverbs: *Jane runs swiftly and Dan dawdles painfully in a yard*. The teacher raps her pointer. 'Pay attention. The orchestra will concentrate.' But heat swarms. 'Look at the oval'—a shrilling student indicates the window's view of stilt-legged walkers. 'You must sit still,' the teacher shouts to the strewn, emptying room.

As You Like It

Mostly it's a problem of memory. There's a man twirling his cane in a familiar film, but you're convinced you've never seen the character before, and the words spoken by the heroine sound like paraphrases from *As You Like It*. Jacques rails, you know the forest must be Arden even as the countryside's referred to by another name, and the words 'A fool! A fool!' bounce in your mind. Though the make of car reminds you of Salinas Valley and a recalcitrant James Dean, you find yourself searching for Rosalind.

Wing

How that feeling, like a wing, held to your body—shifting in thought until the swan was most of what you were; your sense of propriety lifting into lighter edicts, so that air whispered of snow; so that arms murmured of the intimate dance. Your name rested lightly in your mouth; you spoke less often, reading of mythologies that animated the ancient world. Stepping lightly, you thought of childhood privations, heard a crowd breathe appreciation. Thinking of transformation, at last without identity, you were no-one you knew, all wing and a wild idea of flight.

Butter

You don't know the word for *butter*, so you spend seconds miming the way it froths in the pan. The owner of the shop says nothing. You want to buy their famous pesto, but it's nowhere on display. You think of making red sauce and pasta, but *tomato* is another forgotten word. You speak to other customers, who nod and frown. This village's traditions are deeply ingrained; even the postmaster won't leave his mother tongue. Eventually you point at fragrant cheese and a melon that smells of ripest green. How delicious it is—this failure of common names.

Trimountaine

Vestiges; lumps of rock and dirt; the origin of a name. 'We have shaped the earth; filled the bay.' Taming a three-camels' hump of land. *Shawmut*, renamed *Boston*. Blackstone's invitation to fresh water amounting to more than he knew. We remembered *Botolph*, saint of farmers, travellers—a good, worshipping Saxon. Our origins push back into his pious body. We remembered that piety when we hung Robinson and Stevenson, and obdurate Mary Dwyer; remembered, too, our dark journey here—to the bobcats, black bears, moose and coyote. The circles of bats. I chased a chipmunk that was digging my garden. Caught it, was going to pot it. But let it go. Here, where the three peaks were, where the land has been ground. Finding an iota of pity.

Tears

You arrive at the party and a man in a yellow coat thrusts a bag of bananas. Some are green, others are so ripe they appear to melt into the brown paper. You put a green one in your pocket 'for later' and take a glass of champagne from a waiter. A clown is falling over, time and again, as if it's an important joke; three women are juggling fire. On the balcony there are mice on a barbecue. A couple ask about love, flinging themselves against one another. It recurs. You look at the distant glacier that a decade ago filled the land. Melted ice runs into the blue sea as if from a peering eye. Gargantuan tears.

Lozenges

You write from the Protestant Cemetery in Rome: 'I love Keats' headstone; it's taken me back to the poems.' I conjure *The Night Funeral of Jonas Åkerström* and William Story's *Angel of Grief*. When we walked there cats arched their backs and we remembered our original avowals. Oleanders and pines; cool shade like dousings of water. Right words that occupied our mouths. We held loss like bodies in our arms; drank in warm air like breath from the graves. You said love was a forestalling. Over and over, through dark and coughing years: 'And words, too—lozenges in the mouth.'

Fold

The clock folds time into its face. We're looking at a magpie on a wire, raising its wings as if to shape air. A movement of clouds scuffles, until they stand apart, creating space and a bruised aftermath. We touch each other as lightly as the breeze skimming the long grass, as caressingly as a stretched, involving word, gazing at an empty wire, seeing the outline of the vanished bird. We turn from the window and find ourselves stepping through another life, hearing the reverberant cry.

Music

Music is an old Eagles song and your hands are on my body. Was that thirty years ago, hearing my heartbeat like a stuttering engine? Two blackbirds peck at soil in the yard; glossy thoughts line the mind. Your hands are wings as you turn. Your words lift and descend, you sing. A poem you wrote holds for decades, conjuring the sea's sour brilliance. You pointed at pines the size of black thumbprints; gestured at the oblivious expanse. You made up nonsense about being Ophelia. 'An envious sliver,' you said, emphasising the narrowness of the final word.

Ragged Disclosures 4

*They're enamoured of unlikely places—
in Venice, for instance, where paintings
on an apartment's walls hearken after
the Renaissance; where they can't hear
the sound of familiar inflections and a
passageway leads toward the heart of
the building. They follow it, until stairs
drop in unsteady spirals to an ancient
kitchen. Its one window nestles next to
the canal's waters, lapping the
brickwork, and a quotation from Dante
is scrawled on the wall.*

'Amor, ch'a nullo amato amar
perdona,/ mi prese del costui piacer sì
forte,/ che, come vedi, ancor non
m'abbandona.' She reads it slowly,
with misplaced accents, translating it
with kisses, while he watches a boat
slide close to their window—a
shuddering membrane keeping them
from what they nearly touch. 'I'm
saturated,' she says, 'in our murky
love. I can't achieve a clean sense of
it.' At the window, water flusters and
bumps.

'Love spares no-one,' she says. They
climb the stairs to wine-dark light and
a cat occupying their room. It nuzzles
their legs. They've left the apartment
door ajar. In the piazza a band plays
'Vivimi', which she claims 'would suit
Paulo and Francesca.' They sit at the
café and his legs feel weighted, as if
with stones. A sword-thrust of sunlight;
a shout from on the canal. A vaporetto
churns and stalls. The café owner says,
'Someone's found a body.'

TROVE

Music Box

The music box is still in tune, conjuring your
mother's stories of Shanghai's French
Concession and Buck Clayton playing jazz at
the Canidrome—an improbable incantation.
You close the lid. Ghosts are specks in your
eyes, spanning four generations. You offer
cream cake, prepared in the old way;
absentmindedly placing your hand on the
dagger you carried as a child, wrapped in red
silk on the mantelpiece. Escaping the
Cultural Revolution and your parents'
execution,
you hid under muck and straw for three gasping days.

Dancer

Degas' dancer incessantly brushes a fall of
orange hair. Another examines her callused
right foot, feeling years pinch and tighten.
Abstract images, like time—yet as solid as a
pirouetting body. Pigments of orange and
blue; two dancers stretch at the barre. One
picks up a brush; another relaxes her
posture—the dance master finally leaves the
room. A third, trapped by applause, sees a
doubtful shadow
in the wings; a raised, extravagant glass; an imperious hand.

Ship in a Bottle

The ship in a bottle opens the room to gales
and vistas. She tastes salt and cracked lips,
follows her uncle into plumb lines of
narration. Weighted by a store of whisky, he
doesn't surface for days, diving into
intricacies of clewlines and buntlines, finding
murmurous being in the art of glued wood
and miniature decking. He clinks a glass in
tawny light as the ship is rigged. 'Come with
me,' he says, tugging her ear, taking her to
a back room
where wide fleets sail in his incommensurate vision.

Snow

They read Chekhov. Words bring snow and
a view of a tangled orchard. Ghosts haunt the
trees, their own speech fails to catch, the air
is chary of sunshine. Someone is playing
backgammon as centuries weigh—as if
history hangs from their shoulders. In the
next room, a deep voice speaks of a stolen
kiss and pushing through a room full of well-
dressed strangers. They shift pieces around
the board as flurrying wind reminds them the
capital
is many days away; wastes of frozen distance encroach.

Silver

She stirs his tea with the spoon from the flea
market, tapping it twice on the cup's edge,
placing it on the table's pitted Laminex,
asking what they'll do tomorrow. He knows
she'll leave at two in the afternoon, but she
thinks he's unaware of her assignation—they
laugh, and she picks up the spoon, stirring
quietly. 'Are you in love?' he says, hardly
hearing the words escape his mouth. She
scoops a precise half teaspoon of sugar,
dropping it into her already sweet tea. A
breeze shakes her curls as she savours the
Earl Grey. 'So,'
he says, like Solomon ruminating on the disputed child.

Gargoyles

Without guile, diminutive statues that trade in
words of water, we fail to remember our
names. We're children whose souls
hardened. If only we could stretch arms or
marshal sentences. But we live in the stifled
aftermath of prayer, dressed in lineaments of
general fear, spewing awkward notions. Our
gushing eloquence is broken; inclement
weather shouts us
down, even as we shush the closing evening and pretty avenues.

Lantern

She made a shapely dinghy—curved wood, a
hull that bobbed and leaned—but never
rowed it out. She glued an unsteady paper
lantern with slivers of tensed bamboo around
a yellow light. Then strung a necklace from
polished stones, each holding shapes of
wandering water—a slippery, glassy path.
She wore it once
and thought of a freezing creek; of love without accoutrements.

Cradle

Cradled among rocks, the ship's flanks are
torn. The captain's cabin tilts and icy air
jostles the decks like a mutinous crew. The
locals say they'll bring back the store of
caviar in the hold—when the season calms;
when their boats can navigate the crossing.
Last year, four divers were nearly drowned—
tossed like jetsam in the reef-hampered sea.
They saw broken skeletons, rows of jars and
bottles, long cabinets with intricate drawers
and whisky 'by the gallon'. Near the ship the
ocean shines
with a low lustre as of dropped, unobtainable gold.

Her Voice

'Impossible, impossible.' Her voice is a
reed's sound on dark wind, her gait a dancer's
continual misstep. Her eyes are fire in wheat,
distant with the low light that starts in a
haystack. She stretches syllables until they
break. She gathers her long skirts into
clenches, and falls down the hill like a
turmoiled knot or witched commotion. She
says a name over
and over until it makes no sense, staring at the hedgerow.

Ragged Disclosures 5

They're in lockdown in Rome and the neighbours are singing from balconies. Some exchanges are purely comical, such as a man standing on a one-legged stool to perform. 'It's a long way to the ground,' she says, but he never loses balance. Trastevere is otherwise so quiet they return to board games and reading—time and again, as if what they know has lost its scaffold. They imbibe a more opaque knowledge than their language understands.

There's no way through the pandemic's strictures—words won't encompass its implications and government edicts morph every week. Their bodily intimacy's a thousand times refracted; their nouns and verbs speak mostly of the past—as if beginning to dissolve; as if meaning swims away from waists and legs. He inspects weeks of assembled photographs; and music they recorded days ago, and suddenly cannot name them.

'Yes,' she says, affirming a way through negations—'we'll find a way to get home.' It's forlorn at first, but soon they're making a thousand plans while drinking a bottle of spicy Tempranillo. When she stands to stretch, the dome of St. Peter's nestles against her arm— and he remembers her when they met, her blouse draped against a shoulder's curve. For that moment, there was no power in his words.

ISOLATIONS

Your father waits on a park bench, dropping crumbs until the birds are used to him. He tries to discern complexities in their song— like torrid gustings of light. He lifts up those that come close, sensing tenderness in their bony frames and time panting. Sometimes he feels their song on his skin like a faint burring of feathers.

Mud hems the house where a lawn once felted a riverfront. The real estate agent hammers a sign. Earth flakes underfoot and garden beds are spatters of bloom. You buried crockery and dolls' heads, built labyrinthine hose-fed waterways, scratched obscenities into the earth, memorialised pets with plumwood crosses. The purple fruit fell and basketfuls were made into staining, sticky jam. Now you point to a skewed stone wall and pick up a Matchbox Aston Martin. On hands and knees, you propel it at speed.

The trumpeter splits Sunday morning's light. People in the square pay little heed. You're looking skyward as your pram's wheels bounce across cobbles. The southern Italian town falls higgledy-piggledy down a hill, its narrow streets like threads pulled by a needle. After a fractious night you walk to a beach where illicit cargo has long been hauled. The trumpet's notes chase you to a cave's black hole. Fishermen throw lines and speak rapidly, as if exhorting the tide. You nod, opening your hands in the trumpet's mouth, broadcast far and wide.

Your mother spoke as if seizing reality—
turning it over, inspecting its forms, sifting its
iterations. Palpability faded even as you
grasped the household cat; even as your bare
feet flexed on Persian carpet. Latinate forms
intruded. Yet, sunshine startled and birds
shrilled. *Now*—the day opening into staccato
exclamation, disentangled from saying. You
carried yourself toward the river's messy
grammar, untangling nets and casting lines,
dragging 'the catch' in buckets.

You barely notice your body in the mirror. You buy a Portuguese salad bowl and fill it with oranges. The gifts sent by a friend don't suit the space. The apartment has a collection of raucous CDs that match your sense of exigency. You can't say what pulls and presses; what climbs through your spine at night. You make your way toward the city where an Enoteca supplies cheap Tempranillo and a supermarket tray holds ripe artichokes. Outside, your future continues to walk. At night you wake, listening to the footsteps.

Roof beams square the light. The back garden
and cobwebbed studio squeeze toward a
meadow. Your aunt sits outside, on an iron-
framed chair where a rose flickers, refusing
to address her paintings, claiming her father's
violence returns in memory: 'I was three
years old and every day he thrashed me.'
There's bamboo thrusting through lawn;
broken roof shingles; stone walls prised
apart. Your aunt says, 'Buy bananas, cereal
and beans—and a tube of violet.'

Cats adorn an exquisite garden where wind
gathers a pine tree, like an embrace enfolding
a child. A crane hides next to the pool where
koi are as plump as languorous cats; colours
rise in glades of water. You might be stone,
seeing flickers of surface as the crane barely
moves, shifting its head toward another pose.
Each minute buries you further. Someone
speaks but you can't decipher the words.

A clock slows and your uncle's body weakens into a final congestion of sleep. Your sense is of something opening but you can't look at it squarely. Its hands creep across a small stand of beeches; a noise like a ratchet accompanies light. Vocalisations interrupt words. You hear a hum that might be purring light, or shadow, or a slowly failing clock. Beeches are the clock's hands shaken in a fist.

In the studio's yellow haze you see your grandfather. He doesn't look at you but something in the light's colour carries him— as if composed of dust and wood grain; as if his easy way of speaking lifts in motes and breeze. A soft force like his breath on your face; a redolence of skin rising from upholstery. Though he's disarticulated in flame, you lean into his posture.

In the photograph your brother faces the river, chewing gum, fishing and standing under the brown weight of summer. You stand close and apart, occasionally leaning toward his shoulder. He shallow-dives into the water. Weeks after the image was taken he went to live with his father. You've hoped to know him since, but during visits he jams childhood into clipped phrases buried among the rise of stocks and companies—and, when leaving, merely waves. Last week he grimaced and turned his head, looking toward the eroded foreshore. You observe him there—as late afternoon presses on his skin like a damp, warm cloth, watching the pulsing frills of jellyfish, inspecting jags of driftwood, failing to see you.

Ragged Disclosures 6

Even in Trastevere's Botanical Gardens there are unlikely places—where stands of bamboo cluster and sprawl at ragged margins. They hide there from the old city, that's still resuming its form in lockdown's aftermath—as if uncertain of its shape; as if meaning's scaffold sways. Language carries a surlier knowledge than once it encompassed; hands are constrained by edicts about limitation. She speaks with frustrated and insouciant words.

They carry a persistent sense of failure amid climate change and politicians' bickering. Action retreats from public language, as if its words have missed future's chance. But at home she bathes him in talk; carries him on exquisite sentences until excoriation follows—the wordy refraction of their bodies brought back to earth. Mineral and blood begin to swim in verbs and nouns, and they taste each other as if pursuing rituals for the di inferi—those elusive chthonic gods.

'Yes,' she says, in answer to his question about the future. But he doesn't believe they'll recapture their former ways, that are obscure even as he addresses them. Their previous values are tossed; populist ideas are pervasive. Even the notion of excellence is soiled, as if it only belongs to antiquity. She takes him to a museum where ancient Greek sculpture is as sinuous as water: 'If only such hands could refashion this body.'

MANOEUVRES

Jaywalking

The house's walls are crooked as those in Pompeii; a
verandah twists like a brown river. Its chimney leans
northwards. As they grow older an oblique cross-hatching
darkens their nearly identical faces. Part of the house has
collapsed and the garden's a maze of fractured paths and
shrubs. Twice a week they meander to the shops, jaywalking
on roads, traversing parklands. Their sideways-leaning
conversation drags them into lanes and byways.

Flying

Fabric, hands, undressing. A balcony
rail turning. You look to the clock on
the mantelpiece but it's obscured.
What did he ask? Metal ducks climb
a wall. What did you deny? You feel
heavy—flying but failing to move.

Driving

Stare-eyed driving, half-dressed sprawlings on a car seat with backward glances at the Nullarbor, the night sky strewn with verbs. It was a trip you'd promised yourself. Distance crept into your eyes; the desert's orange sand was a contamination. You were distraught three days into the journey, far from any town. He pulled a knife, waved it, walked away from the car. The sun was a black eye. You tried to yoke the parts but they wouldn't hold.

Bouncing

You tug flowers from cracked asphalt, shoo birds, thinking of your grandfather's stories—how, before this highway, trucks ran past with tied and hoisted furniture for further towns; how a limousine brought tall strangers who made the oldest house a museum, drinking champagne until their suicide; how, buried underneath the hill, are acres of glorious multicoloured glass; how the main carpark hides a grass tennis court where your grandfather bounced the ball over and over, twelve times before every serve.

Tipping

Wine tips in a glass—the lemony tang of Sancerre. Cheese
sags on water crackers. You go home. Conversation drifts,
horizons open and grasslands gather a wind's siftings. An
old man at a roadside stall shakes his head as he offers tanned
skimmings of meat, pointing at the sky. Girls spit and yell
expletives from a four-wheel drive. You remember your
marriage, the children you raised. It's as sharp as a hunting
knife. Animal sounds reverberate, and old songs about death.
The grasslands know your failings.

Swerving

Road grit, dust, a swerve and correct
of squealing tyres. On this corner are
the yells of boys, stamped by light.
Haunts under casuarinas; whispers
and stratagems. You mimic the caw
of crows, strutting in their wake. The
old man who fishes has a boxed grin
of hooks. He stands in water hauling
prawns with a hand net. Drowned in
'97 the locals still hear him cursing at
tide's turn. Sand dunes flood the road.

Floating

Angela Hewitt plays Bach's *Goldberg Variations* and her
piano is a raft floating into a river's turbulent centre.
Sensations are a disturbance of glassy-eyed water. It's a set
of stairs to a room where a woman reproaches a man. It is an
intimation of eloquent gods, utterable only in the abstract.
Skin hears; ten fingers are on a spine.

Splattering

You sit on a stone. Dragonflies pull
light, leaves are blotching rain, birds
exaggerate swooping shadows. The
world's a splattering of painter's
pigments, you the tawny yellow the
painter specially prizes, stretching
like a guess of sun on an afternoon
when walking drifted you across a
paddock and burning-off leapt like
feral cats to stain an orchard's
shade—as if a thousand apples
blushed. You sit in water cooling your
hot soles.

Skating

You tried to name the feeling for months, pointing to light skating on the water like a sandpiper's ruff; holding artists from Venetian galleries close to your mouth; finding your face framed by ornate mirrors—yet barely recognising yourself. You were out of your time, eloquent with quotations like necklaces of speech as your lipstick blazoned Henry James and George Eliot. The canals seemed to listen, as if to the remarks of old acquaintances. As sentences curled with the complexity of water, he lay in shadow—your words like an overarching edifice. Ten years later, he smells that green water and remembers your waist decorated with an elaborate band. 'We're not as one,' you said, sending him home. In the plane, he momentarily thought of you as an unheralded angel who'd taught him his insufficiencies.

Walking

You remember footsteps twenty years ago in a market as your boyfriend sought a particular 'classic' CD—that he failed to find. And two days ago, your friend striding up and down in this room. Her father had paced in the same way, repeating a nightly vigil, yet his wife had rarely come home. A way of walking, as if to gather earth's revolutions; or to try to catch the irretrievable. Your friend handled pieces of fruit, stroking them, pressing them to her bosom. She balanced a peach on her palm, rolled an apricot on her cheek. 'Yes,' she said, 'I can easily live without him.'

Ragged Disclosures 7

They're sick of talking. Their sentences
don't even say what happened
yesterday as they argue about an
encounter with a beggar who may have
stolen her shawl. She takes him by the
arms and he relents. Old occasions and
broken promises rise, like bits of river
scrap. He says he thought his parents
hated him. They remember themselves
as separate young adults—unknown to
one another. They undress quickly,
touching skin to skin.

In Rome, they're distant from everyone
else they know well. The city breathes
with the weight of its history; ruins
tunnel beneath modernity's glass.
When they stand in the Sistine Chapel
she recites a passage from the Bible
and a guard shushes her impatiently—
although it's only mid-morning. She
says the art flattens her until she feels
two centimetres tall—such heavy
grandeur and reach. Images and
colours rain, as in an elaborate garden.

'Yes,' she says, wanting to stay for
another few months. She's got to know
the owner of a Trastevere bookshop
and is learning the language. She's
friendly with a luthier, who's making
her a violin. One morning, they walk at
dawn, encountering two naked lovers in
the street arguing about money.
Parodically, the man covers the
woman's breasts with his hands. 'I'd be
like them,' she says. 'I'd drop the
baggage of modesty and prurience.'

SAND

Swan River

We inhabited the Swan River's drifts of salty marshland and
factory waste.   Treacly hours   flowed   through
amphibious summer   as water birds strutted, picking
insects from glitter. We dug sand that became   the Sahara;
waves of hot desert   purled onto Africa's Mediterranean
edge. We rowed bark canoes   through leery jungle,
firing guns at winged shadows.   We pulled sharp-edged
shells from the   pylons   of swimming baths
with bleeding fingers,   washed by rhythms of a mollusc's
somnolent life.

Confusions

Summer lounges on bricks as we cradle dripping glasses
near a blinking window. Morning leans on pulled-back
sheets   and remnant breath.   Soon
we carry   tightening visions in a rackety car across petrol-
smelling suburbs. The sea's blue confusions   douse
and cool; sand is a blaze on crimping feet.   We
suck   green icy poles and watch the sun lumber like
an engine   through the smothering sky.

Billow

Sand was hilly memory, rising in silhouettes. A woman stood against   the undulant shapes, her dress stuttering: 'My island world is ruined'.   A voice pitched low by years, talking of floating a fridge on water, searching for high land, and collecting stones from the seabed— building a wall that the next storm threw down.   She gathered   ancestors'   bones   from   the bobbing tide. We stood with her on this coastline with desert sands rising in   swirls and   shudders. 'Your future arrives,' she said. 'Ours already swims with the fish.'

Enough

The desert tumbles in its sands, the town's a strew of buildings   and   windbreaks. You're out with your lover; night forgets your face in my mirror. Flags clatter   on the government building; there's a tilting dervish of sand;   a woman in labour screams next door.   Your note says, 'enough'. I walk through four rooms, looking at your jeans on the floor and a sock in the hallway. 'Friends,' you said years ago in a London café, and we shook hands as if it were   a pact. You bit your   lip   this   morning,   reminding   me what we're made of, your hands a dance of salient imprecision.

Gale

Windblown sand might be a   distributed
identity, or an   exploded philosophy flying at notions
of being. You can't speak   for yourself   in the withering
gale; can't stand in practiced language's protection. There's
a woman prowling through a house waiting for news of a
lover,   unable   to   reach   him
by phone; there's a man in an alien city trying to remake
himself. The flickering light in a jeweller's reminds him of
his drowned companion and the police   he
evades. His face looks strangely untidy—as if pressed by
fingers   from still malleable   clay.   Now you
wonder   who's speaking even as you hear your voice. You
can't agree with what the voice is saying.

Tunnel

There are closed windows and doors in the mall.
Announcements   on   the   news
refer   to   the   end   of   the   'normal'.
Sand   gusts   remind   you   of   the   beach
where you slid   into   a   tunnel
your   schoolfriend had dug—where you lay   as
wind gathered force and she put her hand on your leg. She
told   you   a   risqué   story
and laughed. You imagine   the beach's vista, remembering
the saltiness of her skin, thinking of the past's
insufficiency—as a grappling wind pushes you into a café.
An old acquaintance is working there and says the café's
about to close.   You see yourself turning away, nodding,
feeling the palpable address of fingers.

Gorse

Sand is underneath my   fingernails and you're
standing at the top of a dune, where gorse curdles and
stiffens, shouting about your parents' neglect. If you were a
disturbance   in the wind I'd duck for cover—
your words rush and darken. Eventually we walk back—for
an hour   through blue evening—until we   barely know
our bodies, the gale dragging us like an airy tide. 'I'd swim
to them,' you say, as if their bony hands still hold your infant
body.   You almost vanish in the fierceness of
utterance—like something liquid   blown about the
oceanic sky.

Bell

In a Tunisian village where water is hauled in buckets; where
the Sahara breathes at night with winds like blown
tarpaulins; where ancient mosaics cling ...
'I'm in love,' you say, as if the word sits uneasily.
You   close   shutters   and   speak   of   secrets.
Women   wail   outside,   one   asking   you
to tend to a wounded boy.   On Sunday as a bell rings, you
dress in the clothes of locals, looking in the mirror at how
your eyes have darkened, outlining your lips with a
forefinger: 'I'm becoming another'. You throw off the
coverlet to expose blue sheets. We   hold
each other   as we remember our bodies in worlds we
belong to. You touch my ribcage: 'A room in which to hide.'

Dune

You said 'no' but the man went ahead and your eyes were the obsidian in a jeweller's window. Weeks later, you followed him and drew a knife across his throat. Desert dunes stood at his hospital window as, in a morphine hallucination, he saw himself buried. The sand's wide frills licked the edges of the building; its passage on night breezes was a repeating accusation. You longed for sluicing, irascible waves, travelling in a bus along a bleached road where traders had moved for centuries, watching a corkscrew of desert wind.

Ragged Disclosures 8

Half-seriously, they make new resolutions. She'll learn the violin; she'll remember ten Italian words a day; they'll walk an hour every morning. It's a regimen for this new European world, but he's lost in the old: sculptures, paintings, novels, philosophies. She says she wants to explain a secret, but stops as she begins, suggesting it's nothing. The shadow of the stalled disclosure hangs in the room—like an eclipse when birds have fallen silent.

'My life's not my own.' They're eating antipasto in Trastevere's Prosciutteria and drinking red wine. He shrugs, as if to say, 'who owns their lives?', but she continues, 'Lily is not my name. My happy childhood's a lie.' They eat silently, as questions brim and tip. 'But who are you?' sounds empty, and she conspicuously fails to answer. They finish the food and walk cobbled streets as confidential strangers.

She says she'll never tell the truth, that they must go on as they are—'lovers who accept one another'. 'Doesn't truth matter?' She says some truths are better left alone. The air between them is a wall and his arms are pinned to his side. 'Lily', he asks when they enter their apartment—'should I still use the name?' She asks whether he cares, pushing him onto the sofa.

THE ARMS REMEMBER

Citrus

Your words have the delicate pith of the citrus—as if
expression conjures a nearly-sweet tea—yet your lips
pronounce meanings that dive like bats from the darkest
sky. One bat is stuck between wires of feeling—I can
neither remove it nor set it free—even as lips conjure
winter jasmine; even as hands spill like mossy water. We
remember ourselves with this kind of speaking—
contradictory, composed of sore feeling. We talk ourselves
into strange fluencies but it won't substitute for the
simplest touch. You're caught by what we cannot express; I
resist what my words clearly imply; the bats are mapping
an invisible place. 'That jasmine,' you say, and fall into
silence.

The Flight of Bats

Thought swerves through images as a bat accelerates
through air. You stand in memory, your dripping shirt
brown from dirty river water; air and sunshine colliding; a
smile lifting your mouth. I'd hold you as I did when you
spoke of thought as knotted and tangled thread; when our
love was umber, arms linking shadowed synapses with
nerve and world. Our tensed bodies were skin-listening
antennae and, as swarming feeling dragged us into air,
night had the colour of dark words. 'I'm there,' you said,
sensation expanding like the sudden flight of bats, sending
ultrasound, tonguing and hearing, sensing gardens and
movement, finding in echolocation the fetching shapes of
night and body.

The Arms Remember

The arms and legs remember. They're fins carrying mind to
the body. A rush of sea; a soft down like a furring of light.
Disentangled words travel perimeters of meaning—melting
adjectives and wayward verbs. The edge of the world's an
old story—in Sappho's poem Tithonus travels there—
where the sea meets the unknown boundary … Standing,
facing the window, seeing a square with four children
playing hopscotch. One chants and throws a cobblestone
like an indecipherable word. A man walks past holding a
cat on a leash. The children point and laugh; the cat turns to
hiss. A body twists on a bed; the sea drops into the room.

Thickening

In Rome, starlings swerve like passages of thought; you stand in awe of thirteenth-century frescoes; we speak cautiously of love—like fugitives. We let the subject drop, walking past Trastevere's sellers of rings and necklaces, near the medieval church. We push arms against our bodies as rain falls luxuriantly and you lift an umbrella, holding it as if touching clouds with its tip. We drink twenty-five-year-old whisky that tastes of caramel and sherry and you say you'd never thought conversation could touch on feeling's limits. In our apartment you open medieval images, pointing out perspectives that, in flattening the figure, 'also reveal it'. Your sentences, like long lines of rain, begin to rewrite my body. You point a finger, tracing bloodlines of language.

Basin

You put your hands in water and stand before the basin
watching turbulence subside. The liquid remains clear and
your gesture imitates a nodding rose. Rain begins; the
window glass lets in the enveloping sound of susurration. It
might be the return of last night's whispers; it might be an
indication of how bodies are enclosed—encircling
embraces that run fluently on skin. You are apart in your
sureness; you will tolerate no diminution—as if early
morning is alert within your eyes; as if a song is climbing
to your lips. You remove your hands from the porcelain as
language opens the world again.

Sidling

A flight of birds; an updraught of air. I watch the estuary
fade; handle my arms, feel your touch on my skin like
drapings of silver water—a few hours, a decade ago. Like a
burr in my gut; a silken savagery. To let go and not be
possessed; to be possessed and never let go. To lie in the
weltering silence, after the rebound of footsteps, knowing 'I
love', not knowing I love, saying to you, 'I do not love'.
And your disapprobation, as if words weigh on your
shoulders and twist awkwardly against your smile. Now, a
rising, like flight, into solitariness; as if the feeling is
mountain-climbing through my body; as if it stands on a
distant promontory. And still the taste and touch you left,
that does not belong, sidling into feeling.

Snared

Snared in language we barely belong to the world. We
press hands to cottage walls and feel the damp, set tinder
and haul logs, light a fire, soak chickpeas, unwrap a portion
of goat's cheese. You scrape mud from your boots. I peel
an orange and mandarin. Wind jerks the shutters. You push
your legs against mine. Language instructs us; our
sensations gather words. You talk of mulching ground and
planting. There are trees in your paragraphs and words in
your ground. There are syllables and tongues in our
proximity. Abstractions caress my hand.

Serpent

I wake as dreams twist and rise, even as daylight quells
them. Words swarm like unnameable creatures, construing
a language of blood and tissue, swimming in flesh and
bones, telling me untranslatable secrets from the body's
lost wordhoard. I'm overwritten, and the palimpsest of my
previous life is fading. A man pushes through teeming rain
to take my arm; a woman names me by strewing flowers.
As she speaks my name, I try its sound in my mouth.

Square

What the rain remembers, we do not know. What our feet
know are millions of steps. What our body knows of
another are obscure passages and extended views; small
rooms and meanderings of conversation. What we feel in
thought has myriad different hues. In my notion of another
I am another person, climbing a hill toward a white-washed
village. A red splash of distant colour is my forgotten coat
in a square.

In That Night

In that night our words flew at the window, close syllables
as unrestrained as birds. Our fingers wandered, as if
counting desire's sum—a number adding up our wanting
years. A delicacy of stuttering lips; a rapid press and pause;
and movement like a bound idea of flight. Syllables
contracted; a kiss examined fluctuations—closing and
opening eyes and gathering us into a second language.

Night

You asked me what the night 'is doing'? I thought of hands
on a thousand bodies and fish pushing through tidal flows;
of both of us together in a strange apartment, clumsily
undoing clothes—fingers tugging on zips and buttons. You
laughed, saying 'we're ridiculous', yet we knew the old
world, with its cobblestones and bowers, looked tolerantly
on ardour. Literature also understands, and though you said
'I could never speak of this', I knew you'd find a way.
Then we dived toward mutual lunacy, cresting through dry
sheets and blankets, like fish that swam into each other,
emerging whole—despite dissolution, despite your question
of what the night might do.

Gown

You're without identity, in this shimmering evening when
the world's a beautiful black gown. I hold you and it's as if
you're night itself, falling between hands. I remember years
ago—we were in a piazza drinking wine; you said you
refused all edicts and exemptions. Those words might be
part of this cascading darkness; until given names no longer
matter; until you're a figure from a story and I'm chasing
the teasing narrative; until the black world swirls with
unacknowledged meanings; until I hold you, here, and you
are a falling black gown.

Pomegranate

Red splashes of sunlight—a ripe pomegranate with spills of
seed; a scarf in Morocco stained with blood. You cradle her
head until she stands up and says 'leave me alone'. The
sun's a lolly on a washed-out cloth as a vendor hoists fruit
on an intricate tray. You're suddenly flushed and have to
sit, thoughts running like animals in an alleyway. Someone
promised to come but won't be here and the injured woman
returns your care, saying 'he's coddled by passion'—as if
love were an egg—and grimaces. The Moroccan translator
waves you off, sunset is splotched on a wide painted board
and your plane points at it like the tip of a brush.

Ragged Disclosures 9

She's packed and says she's leaving tomorrow—action has spoken. He considers her desire for hidden places, that their words have skated over—'my life,' she says, 'is a simulacrum.' Their conversation lacks a scaffold yet hands and eyes still squeeze toward a sort of naming—in the persistent disclosures of their ragged, contriving bodies. 'Tenderness,' she claims, 'remains the best of what we do.'

'All aftermath' is how she construes her life—'everything following my escape.' She won't address the idea of 'before', saturating him in talk like a worried-at distraction—and says when leaving, 'I hope it was okay. I found it better than I hoped.' On that final day they visit a museum and she gestures at a Hellenistic bronze of a damaged boxer in repose—almost as if she knows the man: 'It's beautiful and cruel.'

Although, at first, he wanted more, their shared not-knowing became enough, living with each other's letting-be. She bought a Japanese silk coat, too big for her, and left it as a coverlet on the bed. Sometimes he puts it on, as if dressing in a life that wants to move away, and turns to make the fabric ripple—an eddy in the doubtful world. He hears her as she unbuttoned it: 'Do you know me now?'

Afterword

Prose poetry has found a secure place in the Australian poetry community a century and a half after a variety of French writers first established its central importance to European literature. In many countries, including the United States, the United Kingdom and Australia, prose poetry is now at the forefront of contemporary poetic innovation—evolving in exciting directions, adopting varying formats and techniques and stretching the possibilities of poetic form. This book makes a contribution to understandings of the prose poetry sequence while exploring various consequences and effects of the current climate emergency and the COVID-19 pandemic. It focuses on intersubjectivity and associated themes and issues connected to human intimacy, liminality, the meshing of time and space (including notions of past, present and future) and personal identity.

Acknowledgements

A special thank you to Cassandra Atherton, who made a major editorial contribution to this work. I would also like to thank Michelle Hetherington and our daughters, Suzannah and Rebecca for everything they contributed to the composition of this book. Thanks, also, to Julia Prendergast for inviting me to participate in the Creative Writing/Neuroscience Project, a collaboration between the Australasian Association of Writing Programs (AAWP) and the Science Art Network (ScAN), which prompted me to write some of the prose poems included here. And I owe a great deal to Shane Strange and Recent Work Press for their ongoing support and wonderful expertise.

'Screen' won the 2021 Bruce Dawe National Poetry Prize. Other prose poems were shortlisted for the 2020 Newcastle Poetry Prize and the United Kingdom's 2021 *Aesthetica* Creative Writing Competition (poetry). Various prose poems have been previously published in the *Arc Prose Poetry Anthology 2021*, edited by Pragya Suman; the *Australian Poetry Anthology* (volume 8, 2020), edited by Sara Saleh and Melinda Smith; *Measures of Truth: Newcastle Poetry Prize Anthology 2020* (Newcastle, NSW: Hunter Writers Centre and the University of Newcastle, 2020); *The* Aesthetica *Creative Writing Award Annual 2022* (York, UK: *Aesthetica* Publishing, 2022); *The Incompleteness Book II: Writing Back & Thinking Forward*, edited by Julia Prendergast, Eileen Herbert-Goodall and Jen Webb; *Beltway Poetry Quarterly* (US); *The Ekphrastic Review* (Canada and the US); *Eureka Street*; *Island Magazine*; *Rabbit: A Journal for Nonfiction Poetry*; *Verity La* and *Westerly*. Thanks to all of the judges and editors involved.

About the author

Paul Hetherington is a distinguished Australian poet. He has previously published 16 full-length collections of poetry and prose poetry, including *Her One Hundred and Seven Words* (Massachusetts: MadHat Press, 2021), the co-authored epistolary prose poetry sequence, *Fugitive Letters* (with Cassandra Atherton; Recent Work Press, 2020), and *Typewriter and Manuscript* (Gazebo Books, 2020), along with a verse novel and 12 poetry chapbooks. He has also edited nine further volumes. He has won or been nominated for more than 30 national and international awards and competitions, recently winning the 2021 Bruce Dawe National Poetry Prize. In 2014 he won the Western Australian Premier's Book Awards for the best poetry book published in Australia and in 2017 he was shortlisted for the prestigious Kenneth Slessor Prize. He undertook a six-month Australia Council Residency at the B.R. Whiting Studio in Rome in 2015–16. Paul is Professor of Writing in the Faculty of Arts and Design at the University of Canberra, head of the International Poetry Studies Institute (IPSI), and joint founding editor of the international online journal *Axon: Creative Explorations*. He founded the International Prose Poetry Group in 2014. With Cassandra Atherton, he is co-author of *Prose Poetry: An Introduction* (Princeton University Press, 2020) and co-editor of *Anthology of Australian Prose Poetry* (Melbourne University Press, 2020).

www.ingramcontent.com/pod-product-compliance
Ingram Content Group Australia Pty Ltd
76 Discovery Rd, Dandenong South VIC 3175, AU
AUHW020721050325
407891AU00005B/37